Living on a Mountain

By Joanne Winne

Children's Press
A Division of Grolier Publishing
New York / London / Hong Kong / Sydney
Danbury, Connecticut

Photo Credits: Cover, pp. 7, 9, 17 © 2000 Index Stock Photography, Inc.; pp. 5, 11, 19, 21 © National Geographic Image Collection; p. 13 © Sheldan Collins/Corbis; p. 15 © Alison Wright/Corbis;

Contributing Editor: Jennifer Ceaser
Book Design: Nelson Sa

Visit Children's Press on the Internet at:
http://publishing.grolier.com

Cataloging-in-Publication Data

Winne, Joanne
  Living on a mountain / by Joanne Winne.
    p. cm. — (Communities)
  Includes bibliographical references and index.
  Summary: This book discusses the lives of children who live on various mountains around the world.
  ISBN 0-516-23303-3 (lib. bdg.) — ISBN 0-516-23503-6 (pbk.)
  1. Mountain people—Juvenile literature 2. Mountains—
Juvenile literature [1. Mountain life 2. Mountains]
  I. Title II. Series
  GN392.W56 2000
  307—dc21

                                              00-024034

Contents

My name is Jean-Paul.

I live on a mountain.

I ride a **cable car** to get to my home.

5

My house is on a mountain in the Alps.

Tall mountain **peaks** are all around my house.

7

These men from my town blow **alphorns**.

Alphorns are long horns made of wood.

The horns can be heard from mountain to mountain.

My name is Ang.

I live on a mountain.

My home is in the Himalayas.

11

I live on a farm.

There are **yaks** on our farm.

The yaks give us milk to drink.

13

My brother lives in the **village**.

The village is on a different mountain.

He crosses a bridge to get from the village to our farm.

14

15

My name is Jenny.

I live on a mountain.

My home is in the Rocky Mountains.

I live in a small village on a **mountaintop**.

It is cold and **snowy** on the mountain.

19

There is a lake at the bottom of the mountain.

It is warm on the lake.

I like to paddle my **kayak** on the water.

21

New Words

alphorns (**alp**-hornz) long horns made of wood

cable car (**kay**-bul **kar**) a kind of car that goes up the side of a mountain

kayak (**ki**-ak) a kind of boat that one person paddles

mountaintop (**mown**-tin-top) the top of a mountain

peaks (**peekz**) pointed tops of mountains

snowy (**snoh**-ee) covered with snow

village (**vil**-ij) a small group of houses

yaks (**yakz**) animals with long, thick fur that live in the Himalayas

To Find Out More

Books

Hills & Mountains
by Brenda Williams
Raintree Steck-Vaughn

Living in the Mountains
by Allan Fowler
Children's Press

Mountains
by Seymour Simon
William Morrow & Company

Web Sites
Swiss Embassy for Kids
http://www.swissemb.org/kids/index.html
You can learn about kids who live in Switzerland and the Alps.

Wild-eyed Alaska
http://www.hhmi.org/alaska
Find out more about the amazing animals of Alaska.
You can see animal pictures and play animal movies.

Index

About the Author
Joanne Winne taught fourth grade for nine years and currently writes and edits books for children. She lives in Hoboken, New Jersey.

Reading Consultants
Kris Flynn, Coordinator, Small School District Literacy, The San Diego County Office of Education

Shelly Forys, Certified Reading Recovery Specialist, W.J. Zahnow Elementary School, Waterloo, IL

Peggy McNamara, Professor, Bank Street College of Education, Reading and Literacy Program